WALKER BOONE

CONSCIOUS COACHING

The Ultimate Guide to Starting Your Own Coaching Business,
Discover the Proven Strategies And Tips on How to Make Money
With Your Own Coaching Business

Descrierea CIP a Bibliotecii Naţionale a României
WALKER BOONE
    CONSCIOUS COACHING. The Ultimate Guide to Starting
Your Own Coaching Business, Discover the Proven Strategies
And Tips on How to Make Money With Your Own Coaching
Business / Walker Boone – Bucharest: Editura My Ebook, 2021
    ISBN

WALKER BOONE

CONSCIOUS COACHING

The Ultimate Guide to Starting Your Own Coaching Business, Discover the Proven Strategies And Tips on How to Make Money With Your Own Coaching Business

My Ebook Publishing House
Bucharest, 2021

TABLE OF CONTENT

INTRODUCTION

If you're looking to make some fast cash, or you're interested in building a **long-term sustainable business**, consulting is one of the most lucrative opportunities available online.

As a consultant or coach, you'll be responsible for guiding your students or clients through a learning curve until they've accomplished a specific goal.

The dictionary defines consultant as: *"a person who provides expert advice professionally."*

The truth is, not every consultant is an expert and thankfully, you don't have to have years of experience under your belt to make money in consulting. You just have to know more than the person you are teaching!

Sure, your existing skillset will help shape your consulting business. After all, the fastest way to make money is by offering to teach someone a skill that you already possess.

Another great benefit to consulting is that you can build an income without a major following, or without having access to a massive audience.

This is one of those rare businesses where you don't need a lot of clients to make a full-time income. Just a handful of regular clients will do the trick!

And if you're not yet convinced as to the many reasons why starting a consulting or coaching business is one of the easiest ways to build an online business, there's yet another major benefit to getting involved in this industry.

You'll be able to create a **solid foundation for a future business** that you will be able to **scale as needed!**

The clients who pay you for help, guidance and advice will likely be interested in other services that you offer in the future. Plus, since you'll be working on-one-one with clients, you'll get to know your niche or industry on a much deeper level. This will make it easier for you to create hot digital and physical products that are proven to sell.

You can't build a successful business without a clear understanding of what your market wants. Consulting will give you the insight you need to help them achieve their goals.

And with consultants earning 6-figures a year, it's one of the most profitable businesses to get involved in!

Are you ready to start building a successful business in consulting?

Let's begin!

CHAPTER 1

COACHING BASICS

Synopsis

There are several benefits to suing this style to impart information to others and some are listed below:

The Basics

The coaching exercise may be used to provide for the enhancement of certain specified skills that would otherwise not the available to be masses. This skill can be imparted to the audience through a series of coaching exercises.

Coaching exercises can also tap into the abilities that the individual may not know was within their capacity. The resourcefulness that can be displayed during a coaching exercise can be quite amazing as most of these are done in a need to do basis thus requiring the alertness of the individual hosting the coaching exercise.

Through coaching sessions most participants come away with better confidence levels, more openness in approaching customers and clients alike, more commitment to the tasks at hand, more clarity of the thinking and planning process and a host of other positive traits that can be cultivated through the said coaching experience.

Coaching also helps to enhance the communication skills of the presenter. Through constant practice the communication skills become more finely tuned thus creating a more confident and effective communicator. This is beneficial when the individual eventually has to approach customers and clients to introduce the coaching services to benefit others.

Coaching also helps to empower organizations to be better and more productive in their endeavors. It encourages the participants to work as a team to bring the company to the successes it was designed for. Most companies today engage the services of coaching experts to help motivate the staff periodically.

CHAPTER 2

BUILD YOUR OWN CONFIDENCE FIRST

Synopsis

Although coaching is a very profitable business to venture into, it has to be able to generate certain levels of credibility in both its presentation as well as in its content in order to be recognized as a business entity worth hiring.

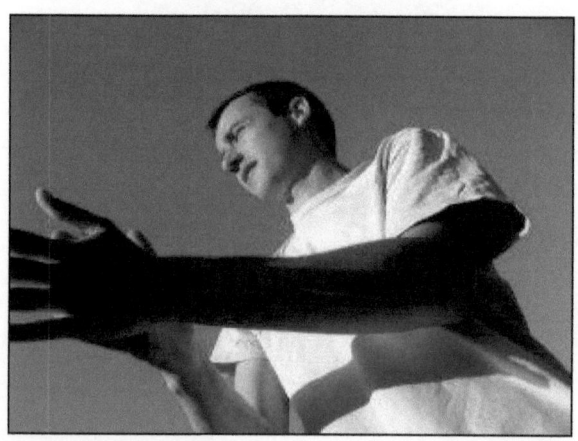

Build It

Having an undisputed or unshakeable confidence level is very important when it comes to making headway in the coaching arena.

In order to adequately hold and keep the attention of the target audience, the coach has to have the presence and confidence to create the aura that is required for garnering the attention of the audience.

The following are some tips on how to build the confidence levels for the eventual purpose of coaching effectively:

Before the actual coaching assignment, working on the material and practicing the presentation will help the individual be more confident in both the material content and also into presentation style.

This practice run will allow the individual to be aware of what the entire coaching programs is about and thus be ready for any elements that may arise during the said session.

Dressing the part will also help to build the confidence levels in an individual. When others look upon the individual with admiration and respect based on the outward "package" presented, the visible acceptance and compliments will help create the automatic confidence stimulation within the individual.

Training to constantly focus on the positive rather than on the negative will also help to build the confidence levels of an individual.

Most people like being around positive minded individual and having this kind of following will be a natural confidence booster which can be tapped into for other needs too.

Making the effort to participate in situations that are not always the individual's forte is another way to build confidence levels, this is especially so when the resulting outcome brings about a positive experience.

CHAPTER 3

LAYING THE GROUNDWORK

Synopsis

You'll begin by identifying your specialties. Again, this doesn't mean you must be a trained expert on the topic. You just have to know more than your clients do.

Survey your skillset. What do you feel you have most experience with? What marketable skills would people be willing to pay to learn? What is your target audience struggling with?

If you're already involved in online business, chances are you have a good idea as to what market you're going to venture into.

If that sounds like you, start by identifying a key problem in your industry and then create a consulting business around **solving that problem.**

If you are brand new to online business, or you haven't yet chosen your niche market, evaluating the knowledge and skills you already have is the best way to start.

Everyone has information that would be valuable to someone else. Whether you're able to teach someone how to master a popular software product, or you know of a way to overcome an obstacle of any kind, that knowledge can be turned into a profitable consulting business.

Kellie Dixon generates over $100,000 a year teaching women how to lose weight by following the LCHF diet. She goes beyond just handing over recipes, because as a consultant she becomes their personal coach, someone who motivates her clients every step of the way while cheering them on throughout their journey.

Kate Riley makes over $10,000 a month teaching new authors how to publish their books on Amazon. She scaled her consulting business to include access to virtual assistants and cover designers, and her clients are more than willing to pay for those resources.

Regardless what you're interested in, chances are there's a wide- open market of clients who need your help. The key is to identify your skills and then validate the market to ensure there's enough of a demand to begin building a clientele.

Knowing what skills you are going to market is key to a successful consulting business.

Begin by asking yourself the following questions:

Are there people already offering your service?

Competition is a clear indicator of a healthy and viable market. If you discover that other consultants are successfully training clients, then you know it's a market worth considering. You just need to find a unique angle that will set you apart.

Are there people actively searching for your topic?

If you see the same questions being asked in your market, chances are, people will pay for help solving their problems. Look for posts on Facebook, Reddit, and twitter from people in your niche. Pay close attention to recurring questions, or requests for help with specific topics. This is a great place to generate ideas for your consulting business.

If you want to dig deep into your niche, you'll also want to join popular Facebook groups. This will put you in close contact with your target audience and help you get a feel for what they're most interested in. It's also a great way to advertise your services later on.

From online businesses looking for help expanding their outreach, HR departments needing help with filling positions, to start-up businesses wanting to build brand awareness, consultants are being hired to help maximize exposure and overall visibility, discover new sales channels and connect with their customer base.

But companies and start-up businesses aren't your only potential audience.

You could easily create a consulting business geared towards the everyday person who wants to learn how to make money online, start a new blog, create an Etsy shop or tackle web design. The possibilities are endless.

Here are a few things to keep in mind when considering your angle:

- What are people actively paying for help with?
- What is lacking in existing consulting services?
- What do people in your market struggle the most with?
- What problems could you help someone overcome that will improve their lives or their business?
- What kind of services can you offer that businesses or people absolutely need, but wouldn't hire someone full-time for?

By answering those questions, you'll be able to find your niche and tailor your services to appeal to the majority of your market.

Once you've identified a need, it's time to start planning your consulting business so you can attract the right clients. I'll show you how to do that in the next chapter.

CHAPTER 4

PLANNING YOUR BUSINESS

Synopsis

Before you land your first client, you'll want to make sure all your ducks are in a row. This includes accounting, business planning and building a web presence.

Consultants need to know basic accounting. You'll need to keep track of the projects you are working on, time spent on each task, and monitor your expenses and client billing.

Consider purchasing a copy of a basic accounting, as well as a project and time management tool that will help you organize, track and monitor your progress.

When it comes to determining a fair price structure for your coaching service, keep in mind that you're limited by how many hours you can spend with clients, as well as how many clients you can take on at any given time.

If you bill $50 per hour and work a 40-hour week, your weekly income would be $2,000. Don't underprice your services, or the value of your time.

It's always best to design a program with a fix cost tied to a specific time frame. For example, $2,000 for 3 months of coaching with 1 weekly Skype call.

This helps you construct a training program that provides all the necessary support, while also holding both yourself and your client accountable for achieving results. It's best to stay away from charging by the hour.

You'll also want to choose a way to process payments while making it as easy as possible on your clients. Many consultants charge at the start of training, while others invoice only after a project has been completed.

For example, if you are offering personalized coaching via Skype or phone, you may want to invoice a portion upfront and then re- invoice for any additional time spent at the end of the call.

For larger projects that require a greater commitment of time, you might want to consider invoicing upfront to protect you from cancellations.

Consider refunds and how you'll handle them. Most consultants don't offer any refunds after the first call, or only a portion of the payment is refunded after the first 30 days.

It's entirely up to you how you handle payments and refunds, but you'll want to plan this out before you land your first client just so there are no issues or misunderstandings later on.

Also, keep in mind that most clients will want printable invoices for tax purposes. You can generate those via PayPal and then save a copy for your own records once it's been paid.

Tip: If you are charging clients monthly, you can create invoices via PayPal that are set to be delivered on specific dates. This will make it easy for you to automate billing, while ensuring that your clients pay on time.

Another thing to consider is how to best utilize contracts. They can help protect your business while laying out what you are offering and what your client can expect.

It's important to protect yourself and your consulting business from difficult clients or constant changes or setbacks that may cost you more time.

Contracts should clearly outline the terms of the project, along with the length of time they are committed to working with you. In addition, you'll want to clearly outline the cost, method of payment and expected billing dates.

You can find fill in the blank templates for proposals and contracts here: https://www.pandadoc.com/consulting-proposal-templates/

Becoming Visible

At the very least, you'll need a website that features your services, and provides insight as to what you can do to help potential clients.

Make sure to include a way for people to contact you, either by phone, Skype or direct email. Most consultants prefer email as it's easier to organize and filter through offers so that you're spending more time responding to the more lucrative ones.

You may also want to hire a graphic designer to create a logo that can be used to help build your brand (this can be featured on letterhead and invoice statements), and set up voice mail so that potential clients can leave messages in the event they are unable to reach you.

CHAPTER 5

CHOOSING A NICHE

Synopsis

For most people venturing into the business arena, some research exercises are usually conducted to ensure its success probability rates are high. Part of this exercise would normally include the identification of the type of business endeavor most suited to the times and expertise of the said individual. This information would then contribute to the decision made regarding the niche market chosen for the individual's business to cater to.

Choose

The following are some tips on how to choose suitable niche markets that can contribute positively to the revenue earning projections of the intended business endeavor:

The obvious way of identifying a suitable niche would be connected to the capabilities and knowledge of the business owner.

Choosing to venture into something that is familiar will give the business owner a better chance of achieving success simply due to the information already known about the said niche market.

Being enthusiastic about the niche chosen will also contribute positively to the business owner, sticking to the choice made. The enthusiasm levels evident will be one of the factors that will enable the individual to face any negatively that might unfold during the business exercise.

Conducting comprehensive market research exercises will also help the business owner make informed choices regarding identifying suitable niche markets to venture into.

The current buying and selling trends factor in very highly in any new business endeavor, therefore careful research should be done to ensure the right choice in made. Failing which would result in a niche chosen that is not only not suitable and sustainable, but will possibly create losses for the business owner.

For those intending to cater to a niche market simply based on the love of a particular product, there is the danger of not being able to look upon the business entity objectively, thus perhaps contributing to a lot of clouded judgments calls.

CHAPTER 6

DO YOU NEED CERTIFICATION

Synopsis

Although most coaching establishments are certified in some form or another, it is not always a pre requisite for those intending to acquire the services of the coaching expertise for their staff.

What Do You Need

The coaching business covers a very diverse area thus being competitive and staying on top of the completion is more likely to get the bulk of the coaching business entity rather than pursuing accreditation and certifications.

Most coaching platform relies on the visibility its content creates and also on the positive feedback given from satisfied clients. This will also create to desired advertising angle for the coaching business, as satisfied customers make the best advertisers.

However, having the relevant certification does help when one is intending to cater to the more intellectually savvy platform. Those in this caliber expect to be on the receiving end of information, based on the presenter having the relevant credentials to back up or support the material being presented.

This can also be used for advertising purposes where the target audience is enticed to attend the coaching session based on the perceived expertise to be gained by the accredited speaker.

When it comes to getting the relevant licensed for the business there is also the need to have the proper certification to show the legitimacy of the material being offered through the coaching experience.

Most endorsing committees will only give their approvals based on the certifications the business entity can produce.

This certification also ensures the general public or would be clients, that all the services being offered by the business entity is done so from acquired training skills form reputable sources. This will also assure the client that the material being used is both legally endorsed by the relevant governing agencies and also by the bodies that monitor such material.

CHAPTER 7

SETTING FEES

Synopsis

There are several factors that govern the fees setting structure for coaching. These are usually dictated to be the current market trends and the materials being offered. In order to be able to set a fairly competitive and acceptable fees structure there is a need to first evaluate the current market trends.

What To Charge

The following are some tips on how to decide on the fees setting structure:

The expertise and experience of the presenter or coach makes a big difference in the charges that can be imposed. If the individual giving the coaching session is well known and an accepted authority in the field being presented than the fees charged can and usually is considerably higher to others making the same of similar presentations.

The area being explored at the coaching session also has some bearing on the fees that can be charged. If the topic is considered popular for the current market trends, then the fees charged would also reflect this, and it is commonly accepted to be also higher when compared to other topics.

This is also true when it comes to charging higher fees for niche areas where the materials and the experienced presenters are quite limited.

The length of the coaching agreements is also another point taken into consideration when fees are being decided.

If there is a contract in place to provide coaching services over a lengthy period of time, then the fees charged will reflect the continuous commitment on the client's behalf.

Fees are also decided based on the need to have any other added services that may complement the existing coaching exercise.

These may include personalized attention of a smaller group, further in depth coaching needs and any other modules that the client may deem fit for the company's overall optimum progress.

Any or all of these fees does really follow any rigid structure and is usually open for discussion, to best accommodate both coaching establishments and prospective clients.

CHAPTER 8

GETTING CLIENTS

Synopsis

In every business there is the ever present challenge of getting and keeping clients. There are several contributing factor that ensure both scenarios are acquired however some effort has to be exercised in doing so.

Customers

The following are some of the areas worth exploring if the business entity is looking to widen the client base and expand the company:

Visibility – this is the most important element that deserves a lot of effort and thought. Without this visibility element it is very hard for the business entity to be able to attract the customer base desired.

Therefore all means has to be explored diligently to ensure the best tools are used to create this visibility effectively and easily. There are both online and offline tools that can be used to effectively promote the business and some of these are quite cost effective is not altogether free.

Advertising the capabilities of the coaching establishment without actually stating its limitations if any is an effective way to get the target customer base interested enough to make the initial contact.

There is no real need to divulge all information especially when it is less than attractive as a selling point. Clients are more inclined to focus on their needs and whether these needs can be provided for by the coaching entity hired.

Therefore hard selling these, to get the client convinced of the potential services provided will be a better idea than simply listing all the coaching featured capabilities.

Taking the trouble to understand the market needs and the client's needs will help the coaching business design packages to appear more attractive and applicable to the customer base.

This is an effective way to garner the attention of the prospective clients as they will be assured to hiring a coaching entity that specifically suits their needs.

CHAPTER 9

USING A TRIAL SESSION

Synopsis

This is a relatively new style of "advertising", but is none the less very effective; as the client is able to view firsthand the quality of the work the coaching company is capable of extending.

Trail

There are a lot of businesses today that go the extra step in providing free samples of their products in the hope that a fraction of the intended customer base can be made to commit to an eventual purchase based on the trial offered.

This same method is being adopted by companies that are in the service providing business, where free trials are offered so that companies can actually have the opportunity to try out the services and then make better and more informed decisions as to the merits of the service offered and its corresponding costs.

Bearing in mind that this system only works when the intended product or service extended has the positive qualities that will ensure and even guarantee a commitment from the free trail extended.

The coaching free trials should also be able to deliver optimally designed product content to ensure the same positive commitment from the potential client.

The trial session extended is usually designed to take on the form as a teaser to the actual full module used in the training sessions.

These teasers if designed well should have all the features that are attention grabbing and technically beneficial to the participants in order to ensure they will be more than willing to commit to attending future paid sessions.

These trial sessions are also a good way to get the company through the preliminary stage of getting the client's attention.

When it comes to promoting a business, most people are not savvy enough to lock in the prospect interest from the very onset of the meet, therefore providing "free" trials will comfortably create the leverage needed to make the first meeting potentially beneficial to both parties.

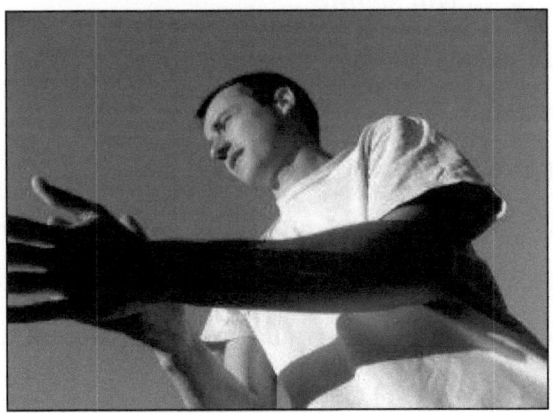

CHAPTER 10

LANDING YOUR FIRST CLIENT

Synopsis

Once you've created the foundation for your consulting business, it's time to start recruiting new clients.

So, where do you begin?

One of the easiest ways to land your first client is to focus on **building a list**. Your list is a powerful sales tool, and it'll help you better connect with your target audience.

You can begin building a mailing list by creating a simple blog that provides valuable information, posts and articles. Demonstrate your commitment to helping your market, while also highlighting your expertise.

A well-crafted blog is one of the most powerful ways of building a foundation for your consulting business. It serves as a launch pad and helps connect you with potential clients without cold calling or hard selling.

Your objective should be to publish 2-3 posts a week that tackle different problems your customers are facing. Don't be afraid to over-deliver, your content won't take away from the potential to land clients. Most people prefer one-on-one coaching because they need more help or crave personal guidance.

If you want to give your blog visitors an easy way to download your posts and content so they can refer to it later (helping your brand become memorable), you'll want to grab a copy of Post Gopher, available at: https://postgopher.com/

Post Gopher is a Wordpress plugin that lets your visitors save a copy of your content in PDF format so they can read it later, or share it with others.

If you aren't interested in creating or maintaining a blog, you could always design a landing page that offers a free incentive to those who join your mailing list. This is an easy way to capture leads while providing value.

Make sure your incentive offer is exclusive to your website. Don't use white label content unless you've repurposed it in order to represent your brand and reflects your personal style.

Short reports that provide step-by-step action plans, how-to style guides or even full length eBooks are all fantastic tools at persuading visitors to subscribe to a newsletter. And of course, video content is always in demand.

You can easily create a landing page as well as build and manage your mailing lists with one powerful tool available here: http://www.ClickFunnels.com

And yet another powerful strategy that consultants use to connect with their audience and identify potential clients is to create a simple membership site that provides access to a handful of free tools.

Membership sites are **proven winners**. People look at them as holding tremendous value because the content isn't freely available. They need to create an account to gain access to the material.

When you're just starting out, you'll probably want to create a free membership site so that you can quickly build your list while pre-screening potential clients who take action by subscribing to your site.

It also gives people a sense of community and that they are part of your tribe!

Plus, you can then take advantage of scarcity by offering only a certain number of free membership accounts. Create a sense of urgency and you'll convert those visitors into subscribers easily.

Here are a few quick and easy methods to help you get started:

Social Media:

I've seen consultants land their first client just by creating a Facebook page or group around their business and then promoting that page through Facebook ads.

With Facebook advertising, you can customize your ads to be seen by specific demographics (new business owners, etc.), making it easy to get your business in their line of sight.

Facebook groups should offer something of value before you try to sell your services. Consider setting up a support group for your target audience so they can discuss the market, ask questions and share information with each other.

Then, once your group has become active, you could begin to advertise your one-on-one consulting program! It's a great way to position yourself as an authority figure in your market, while connecting with your target audience and offering them value just by being part of your tribe.

Paid Advertising:

There are countless paid advertising opportunities available to you, including promoted pins or twitter ad campaigns but one of the most affordable methods of reaching your audience is investing in paid newsletter ads. Plus, being featured in a newsletter can serve as an endorsement of your services!

Find Clients through Linkedin:

Many businesses turn to LinkedIn when searching for potential consultants, so don't overlook this powerful method of connecting with clients. Create your account and make sure to include relevant keywords in your bio so you appear in on-site search queries. You'll also want to include a link to your social media profiles and your website's service page.

If you can get endorsed by past and existing clients, former employers or networking partners, make sure to add those to your connections. The more recommendations you receive, the better.

CHAPTER 11

TEACHING OTHERS TO BE A COACH

Synopsis

When the coaching business does well there may be a need to extend the coaching staff to accommodate such expansions. Such expansions may need the expertise of having to coach others to take on the responsibilities.

Helping Others

The first thing to ensure is that the proper tools are in place to help the teaching session go smoothly so that the intended material to be imparted to the new coach, will be absorbed as it is being taught. Such tools should also be available to show the "students" how to teach using these tools.

Besides the actual material being imparted, there is also a need to ensure the chosen individual has the charisma and confidence needed to be an effective coach. Providing them with motivational material and constantly reassuring the "students" with positive reinforcement will allow the individual too slowly and surely develop the confidence needed to portray a well adjusted coach.

Part of learning how to be a good coach is also the ability to observe and relate to the audience during the coaching sessions. This is an important observation to make as it will give the coach an idea of how well received the presentation is.

It will also allow the coach to make the necessary adjustments to ensure that the time spent at the coaching session is beneficial to both the coach and the participants.

WRAPPING UP

If you want to make money in consulting, you need to sell results, not hours. You're catering to a client's need for guidance and information, so you want to provide them with a clear outline of how you'll help them achieve their goals.

Your clients will expect to walk away from your coaching having been improved in some way, whether it's on a personal level such as with a weight loss or self-help mentoring program, or on a professional level, if you are offering skill-based training services.

Successful consultants understand that a successful business relies on trusted relationships and open communication with clients.

Be clear with the times you are available so that your clients come to know they can depend on you, while still respecting the fact you have a life and won't always be available.

Don't make promises you can't keep. And most importantly, always follow through. The more you treat your clients with respect and do everything in your power to provide them with the service you've offered, the easier it will be to build long-term contracts.

Word of mouth referrals is a powerful method of expanding your business, so treat every client as if they are your only one.

Printed by Libri Plureos GmbH in Hamburg, Germany